Humbled

Mental Health, Addiction and Christian Poetry

David LaChapelle

The reward of humility [that is, having a realistic view of one's importance] and the [reverent, worshipful] fear of the Lord Is riches, honor, and life.

Proverbs 22:4 (Amplified Bible)

POEMS

A neurotic is a man who builds a castle in the air. A psychotic is the man who lives in it. A psychiatrist is the man who collects the rent.

Jerome Lawrence

Rebuked

Went to the Shrink

Knowing I am weak

Worn out from life

Did not get my own way

Took its toll on me

Bowed down on bended knee

Could not see the forest for the trees

Walked in the office

Knowing I am guilty this time around

Full of sin

Burdened beyond compare

Masking a frown

My appearance did not tell lies

I could not hide

Dr. T looked at me

With examining eyes

She saw right through my disguise

Dr. T rebuked me without scorn

A good man when being told

Is happier than before

Someone cared

To start a new day

Life now has meaning

I am not doing this all by myself

I can keep on believing

For the good to be

And for me to appreciate

The beauty of being alive

For the first time in a long time

Reorder

At the end

Of struggling within

Accepted my fate

That I am late

Lost the battle

Cannot go any further

Without a reorder

Victory is mine

The war is won

Before time

Going through the motions

Got old

Need to be told

Went to Dr. T

She showed me

What I thought was real

So surreal

Now a new deal

Sent from above

Full of love

Happy

I got my pills

Now I can chill

Float the day away

In peace and harmony

Nothing bothering me

No thoughts going astray

Emotions kept at bay

Leaving me found

Not making a sound

Content and happy

Hooray!

It was tough

To get through the rough

I made par

I made it this far

Only a miracle

Trust you Lord

Whatever for

New Deal

Sin lost its appeal

I have a new zeal

Now I can feel

What is real

Dug up the roots

That had no fruits

Dead branches

Breaking the fences

Brought down in time

Walk the line

Everything is fine

Hope it lasts

So sublime

<u>Help</u>

When trying to say

What I cannot say

What I do not say

Is what I say

Read between the lines

Uncover my crimes

False identity inside

Always trying to hide

Need a helping hand

To be a better man

Help me believe

In myself once again

Through the lies I tell myself

That are not from above

Reaching Out

Face the day

Do what you can

Be a better man

No pressure

Move forward

Accomplish something small

Hope for an open door

The best for all

Only way to stand tall

Make a call

Reach out for help

It is okay to yelp

I love you David

Dependent

Cannot believe what I feel

Cannot believe what I see

Cannot believe what I think

Cannot believe what I hear

Only your spirit

Gives me spiritual discernment

To grasp the truth

Clarity and understanding

Protecting my steps

Guiding my life

In need of help

Crossroads

Cannot be trusted with beer

One is too many

A hundred is not enough

Give up excuses

That I need to drink

Like it helps me sleep

I have got to quit

Sobriety will be alright

It is His plight

Not my might

To take flight

Not live in regret

Break the chains of bondage

Not hurt my testimony

Be a better man

Resolution

Gave up beer

Up at night to glare

At the words on this page

I feel like a sage

Need to lose weight

Eat half on my plate

Focus on what matters

Leave a lesser shadow

Makes a better man

Must make a stand

What can I say?

That is my reality

Today is today

Leaping

Discern what is good

Discern what is not

Sober this time

Make a wise choice

More than saving the pocketbook

See how long I can last

No pressure

Something has to change

God has to come through

I will do my part

For a better day

For all involved

The rest is up to you

Help me pull through

Other Side

Sober up

Be the light of day

Have something to say

Backed by overcoming

Grace overflowing

Come my way Lord

To an open heart to play

Start a new day

Do not do it

There is another way

Hope

Come to the end

Nothing to win

Hit the bottle

Full throttle

Playing the fool

Ensnared so soon

Did not take a long time to sin

No way out

Promise to change

For a better way

A brighter day

Do what I can

Christ will do the rest

Answer

So many strongholds in my mind

Broken to pieces before my eyes

Thoughts and feelings I once had

Smashed into the abyss

Of what does not last

Gone forever

I am a new man

What can I say

He has a plan

Viewpoint

So many ways to look at things

So many angles to wrestle with

A matter of perspective

To be renewed

Seek the good in the world

A testimony of His love

Whatever is going on

Is the only way

To be ok

The Lord is control

He loves us

Everyday

Salvation

Don't have what it takes

To win this race

Handle striving against sin

On my own

Want to understand my plate

You are more than that

Can anyone relate?

Struggling to hold it together

Saving my own skin

Is a tall order

Jesus is the compensation

Here to proclaim the good news

Do not be left behind

And snooze

Lost

Feelings are not important

Working for Christ at the forefront

Saving souls for Jesus

Bringing the harvest into the storehouse

The fruit is ready to pick

The time is ripe

To prepare the table for dinner

Welcome Him in your heart

Sit down and feast

With the rest of us

Is a start

Near Time

Days shorter

Nights colder

Seasons change

Harvest time is here

The Lord's return is near

Prepare yourself for His Grace

To surround your heart

These last days

There is no other way

Heaven awaits

Come as you are

He will restore you

He wants to love you

Forevermore

To Belong

Life's rollercoaster ride

A lot of ups and downs

Not made to stand

This time around

Skipping the judgment

Forgiveness of sins

The gift of life

Extended to us

Christ living in me

The rest is looking up

Where we belong

For Eternity

Light

His Word is enough

For all my stuff

Selfish and limited

Helpless not hopeless

Darkness to light

Shining bright

Manifesting in peculiar ways

Coming alive before my eyes

Arranged so skillfully

The Lord's master hands

We are made in His image

So glad

New You

The time has come

For the setting of the sun

Righteousness on display

Run over with His love

Turning you to change your mind

Manifested truth

His heart coming to you

Cannot reason it out

The Lord will show you

What to do

Now is the best time to be

Give your life to Christ today

Don't delay

There may not be another day

Decision

Harvest time is here

Set your clocks behind

Move quickly

He will not be long

More than choosing the Lord's will

In the storm

Life over death

Doors open not closed

There is still time to settle the score

The ball is in your court

Don't believe the father of lies

Satan in disguise

Fast Return

The time has come

For the setting of the sun

Truth will be made clear

After creation buzzes out of here

Too many things to distract

One event to the next

That is how he works

Opposing forces

Hold on for dear life

The Lord is coming fast

To rescue those who believe

Do not be left behind

See the fulfillment of destiny

That cannot be erased

On that glorious day

Waiting

Finish strong

Discouraged in the storm

Oh Wait!

Refreshed by the waves

Be blessed

A second chance

A second wind

To do life with Christ

Coming home is on my mind's eye

Too crazy to stay

Jesus will pluck us

out of this mad discourse

Just wait

He will not be late

A Calling

Serious times

Thank God I am alive

Should have been gone long ago

God had a plan for me to sow

Made strong to fight

To save the lost

Not in my own strength

To trust in His might

That the message would reach new heights

A relationship forged by necessity

He brought me to know what is necessary

All His

I am free

It was my pride

Took me for a ride

Did not think I would make it

Trying to fake it

Gave up the fight

To keep holding tight

What I was afraid to lose

Was not real anyway

God welcomed me in

When I surrendered to Him

No way to win

Any other way

Humility is the key

To fill me up with glee

Giving Up

Take away my thorn

No more scorn

Early in the night

Full of fright

Arguing with God

To see my point of view

To come on board

And finish this review

Realized not going win

Must be another way

What is God speaking to me

Through the purpose of this pain

I give all of me to you Lord

I lay down my sword

I see that was you all along

Now in clear view
I am new

Love

God is Love

I see the pain was not you

My pride needed to come unglued

There is nothing to subdue

Adversity was tearing me down

You were building me up

At the same time

Empty me out of me

Fill me up with you

Through the crushing, molding and shaping

Of my soul

My character forevermore

I know your faithful now

You were loving me all this time

Chastised

Adversity

You kept me close

I got to know you

Drawing out of me

My pride

I could not hide

Had to come to the end

Of struggling within

I see it was all you

Denying me from rising so soon

Protecting my steps

I was a danger to myself

A short leash

Felt suffocating

Now I can breathe

<u>Real</u>

Humbled by dependency issues

I am limited not a victim

I know my value

In Christ's currency

Worth more than silver and gold

He chose me before I was in my mother's womb

You revealed yourself to your servant

Now aware of your faithful stare

I see you were loving this child

I trust you

You are real to me

Content

Will you take me home Lord

Before the proper time

I am human

Need reassurance

Why am I holding on

To what is passing by

This world is all I know

Hope for something better

Embrace new avenues

Being Christlike is the goal

Be a testimony to show others the way

Cannot fathom anything else

Count my blessings

I am sorry

I like feeling this peace

<u>Exam</u>

I passed God's test

This time around

How do I know

I am moving forward

Taken a million times

I am a slow learner

A wandering sheep

Closer to Jesus

What will I face

Open arms to embrace

The blessings and be raised

Hopefully the war is over

The final stage

Dues Paid

You are the warden

Release the prisoners

Set the captives free

You paid my ransom

Blood on the cross

It all started with Adam

You would not let me go

I am glad

You put up with me

Patient and kind

If you did not lead

Through the valley down low

I would not know you as well as I do

Ruled

Fighting for the sake a fighting

Had to come to an end

Burn itself out

I cannot win

God has a better hand

Trumped me every time

Letting me go on

Putting on a show

At the right time

He stepped in

Intervening with His love

Grace the evidence

I was made for Him

Knowing that now

Open the floodgates

Water my soul

Lost Agenda

Lost my agenda

It feels great

To know Jesus more than I did

He kept me on a string

He knew of better things

Dismantling my defences

Revealing Himself to me

I am blessed to be His

I wish everybody felt the same

I guess you have to be chosen

It is a decision you can make

It is all relative anyway

Come to Him

Jesus will take you in

<u>First</u>

Freedom

From the bondage that enslaved me

Everything is clear

Empty vessel to steer

My redemption draws near

Ashes for beauty

Filled with His love

To be exalted above the rest

The last is first this time around

It is going to be permanent

We believed

That is why we see

What is happening today

Is no surprise to us

Rapture

Born with a fallen nature

Did not like my sentence

We are all on the same train

The narrow pathway

Taking us to the same place

We who believe

Will live for another day

Down here is the school yard

Where we develop His magnificence

Heaven will be the greatest escape

ABOUT THE AUTHOR

David LaChapelle is a born-again Christian since the year 2000. David has earned himself two Computer Technical Diplomas from Seneca College, in Toronto, Canada in 1994 and 1996. He graduated with a Psychology degree in 2011, from Trent University in Peterborough, Canada, where he now calls home. David lives a quiet life and enjoys writing and being an author. He is proud of his works, and hopes it will bring him recognition in this life and rewards hereafter. David is a firm believer in reading the Word of God, and the power of prayer and wishes the best for all humanity awaiting the Lord's return.

OTHER BOOKS BY DAVID LACHAPELLE

David's Adventure with Schizophrenia: My Road to Recovery

David's Journey with Schizophrenia: Insight into Recovery

David's Victory Thru Schizophrenia: Healing Awareness

David's Poems: A Poetry Collection

1000 Canadian Expressions and Meanings: EH!

David's Faith Poems: Christian Poetry

Freedom in Jesus

Canadian Slang Sayings and Meanings: Eh!

The Biggest Collection of Canadian Slang: Eh!

Healing Hidden Emotions for Believers

Breaking Clouds: Christian Poetry

Walking Light: Christian Poetry

Let Go: Christian Poetry

David's Faith Poems II: Christian Poetry

Eternity Calling: Christian Poetry

Receiving Grace: Christian Poetry

All books and e-books available at Amazon